GOOD GRIEF,
CHARLIE BROWN!

Turn this book over for
FOR THE LOVE OF PEANUTS!

by Charles M. Schulz

GOOD GRIEF,
CHARLIE BROWN!

by Charles M. Schulz

Selected cartoons from
GOOD GRIEF, MORE PEANUTS, Vol. 1

FAWCETT CREST • NEW YORK

GOOD GRIEF, CHARLIE BROWN!

This book, prepared especially for Fawcett Crest Books, a unit of CBS Publications, the Consumer Publishing Division of CBS Inc., comprises the first half of GOOD GRIEF, MORE PEANUTS!, and is reprinted by arrangement with Holt, Rinehart, and Winston, Inc.

FOR THE LOVE OF PEANUTS!

ISBN: 0-449-23027-9

Printed in the United States of America

First Fawcett Crest printing: May 1974

16 15 14 13 12 11 10 9 8 7 6

GOOD GRIEF,
CHARLIE BROWN!

KRINKLE

IT SAYS HERE THAT IF A DOG'S NOSE IS WARM, HE PROBABLY ISN'T FEELING WELL..
VERY INTERESTING...
I WONDER IF SNOOPY'S NOSE IS WARM OR COLD?
WHY DON'T YOU FIND OUT?
?
YOU MEAN TOUCH HIS NOSE?! OH, NO...I COULDN'T DO THAT...OH, NO....I'D BE SCARED...
YOU MEAN WALK RIGHT OVER, AND TOUCH IT, DON'T YOU? OH, NO...I DON'T THINK I COULD EVER.. I'LL DO IT!

TUM DE
TUM
TE DA
TE DUM ♪♫

SCHULZ

HERE...TAKE A CARD...ANY CARD..

ZOOM!

NO, NO, SNOOPY! NOT THOSE!!

WHAM!

BOY, WHAT A STUPID DOG!

SCHULZ

WHEEEEEEE

SCHULZ

Now turn this book over,
and read
FOR THE LOVE OF PEANUTS!

Now turn this book over,
and read
GOOD GRIEF, CHARLIE BROWN!

I SAID, 'MAYBE'.

OH, WELL...IT'S KIND OF NICE TO BE FREE AGAIN!

YOU'RE THE ONLY PERSON I KNOW WHO CAN USE UP A WHOLE DAY IN FIVE MINUTES!

KLUNK!

SCHULZ

THUMP THUMP THUMP THUMP

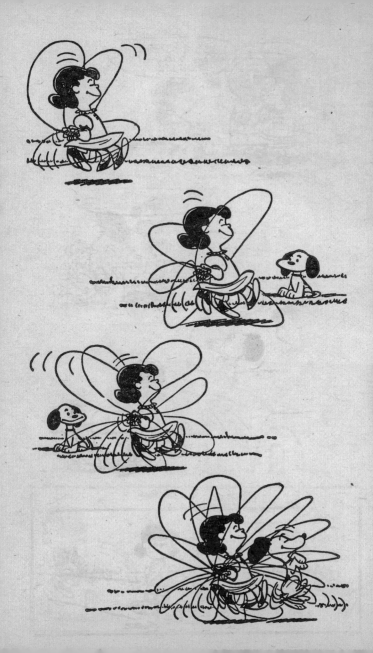

HOW CAN I TAKE YOUR PICTURE IF YOU'RE GOING TO SIT 'WAY OVER THERE? COME UP CLOSER..
NO, NOT THAT CLOSE! MOVE AWAY!
NOW DON'T, SCOWL, SNOOPY, PLEASE!
AND DON'T GIVE ME THAT SILLY GRIN!
AND DON'T TURN YOUR HEAD! LOOK AT THE CAMERA!

FOR THE LOVE
OF PEANUTS!

by Charles M. Schulz

Selected cartoons from
GOOD GRIEF, MORE PEANUTS, Vol. 2

FAWCETT CREST • NEW YORK

FOR THE LOVE OF PEANUTS!

This book, prepared especially for Fawcett Crest Books, a unit of CBS Publications, the Consumer Publishing Division of CBS Inc., comprises the second half of GOOD GRIEF, MORE PEANUTS!, and is published by arrangement with Holt, Rinehart, and Winston, Inc.

GOOD GRIEF, CHARLIE BROWN

ISBN: 0-449-23027-9

Printed in the United States of America

First Fawcett Crest printing: May 1974

16   15   14   13   12   11   10   9   8   7   6

For the Love of Peanuts